T3-BPD-457

HORSES

written and photographed by Ruth S. and Ed Radlauer

Bowmar Publishing Corp./Glendale, California

International Standard Book Number: hardcover 0-8372-0374-0 softcover 0-8372-0373-2
Library of Congress catalog card number FiA68-4643

First Printing .... November 1968
Second Printing .... February 1970
Third Printing .... October 1970
Fourth Printing .... July 1971
Fifth Printing .... July 1972
Sixth Printing .... April 1973

How do you like Robin's big pet? He's named Sam. Robin got him when he was just a baby, a *foal*. When he was very young he was called a *colt*. Now he's a six-year-old.

This mare is proud of her baby girl, a one day old *filly*. Foals can stand up as soon as they are born. Colts and Fillies stay with their mothers for about six months.

Jay Boy is a proud colt. He's only ten months old, but he can be dangerous. You see, when Jay Boy gets scared or *spooked,* his feet hardly touch the ground. When he gets spooked, watch out! It means danger.

Colts and fillies don't go to school, but they do need training. You might like to ride Red some day, but not today. His owner, Lyn, knows Red has a lot to learn before she can ride him. Sometimes it takes a year to train a horse.

Sam lives in a corral. It's a pretty good place to live because Robin keeps it clean. Having a horse is fun, but it also means hard work. The work goes faster when friends help each other.

Horses must have hay and water two times a day. Robin carries hay and fills Sam's water bucket every morning and night. Maybe sometimes there's enough rain to fill the bucket, but you carry hay, rain or not.

When the rain stops, Robin takes Sam out for training. Sam might spook when he sees something new and strange. Robin talks to Sam and lets him look. To us it's a pile of junk, but to Sam a pile of junk may look strange. After they look the ring over, it's time to train.

Robin tells Sam what to do as they go around the ring. She may say *walk*, *jog* or *lope*. A walk is slow. A jog is like a trot, and a lope is even faster. To stop, Robin says, "Whoa!" When Sam hears "Whoa," he puts on the brakes.

Before she rides, Robin cleans Sam's hooves with a hoof pick. That's like a tooth pick for hooves. She also brushes his coat and combs his mane and tail. He never had it so good! Who *said* horses aren't smart?

Sometimes friends ride together. Joan's horse, Banner, is Sam's friend. Banner always wants to race, but Robin won't let Sam race.

She says, "Sam, you get too excited, and when you get excited, you sometimes buck."

Here is a trail course where riders make their horses go through obstacles. Robin backs Sam through this trail obstacle. He can't look back so she tells him how to go by pulling back on the reins and steering him with her legs.

Grooming the horses keeps the girls busy. Grooming means Sam gets a clipping, a bath, and a lot of combing and brushing. When you are clipping, stay away from Sam's ears! If you don't, you may land on your own ear.

What a horse must do to please his owner! The water's cold! But Sam likes it when Robin scrubs his back. The bath and combing and brushing will make his coat shine. Does all that grooming make you wonder where they're going?

They might be going to a horse show. At a show you see all kinds of horses and many different events. Jumping is an event that's fun to watch. Do you see why riders in jumping events must wear hard hats?

There is a very old story about a horse that could fly. That horse named Pegasus had wings. This horse almost flies without wings. Would you call him Pegasus?

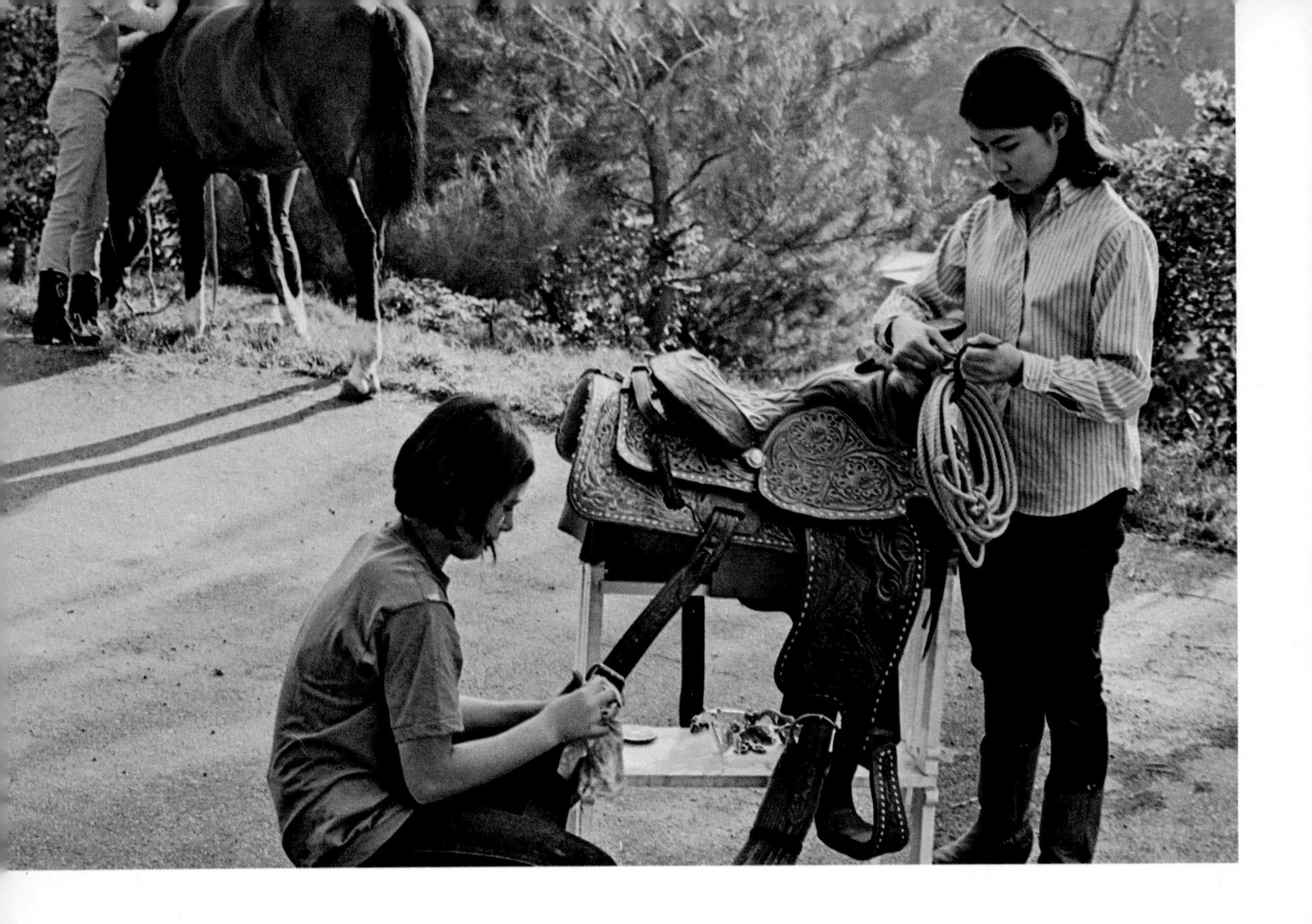

After the grooming the girls get ready. Robin cleans her saddle with saddle soap. Joan ties a rope on the saddle. It surely looks like horse show time!

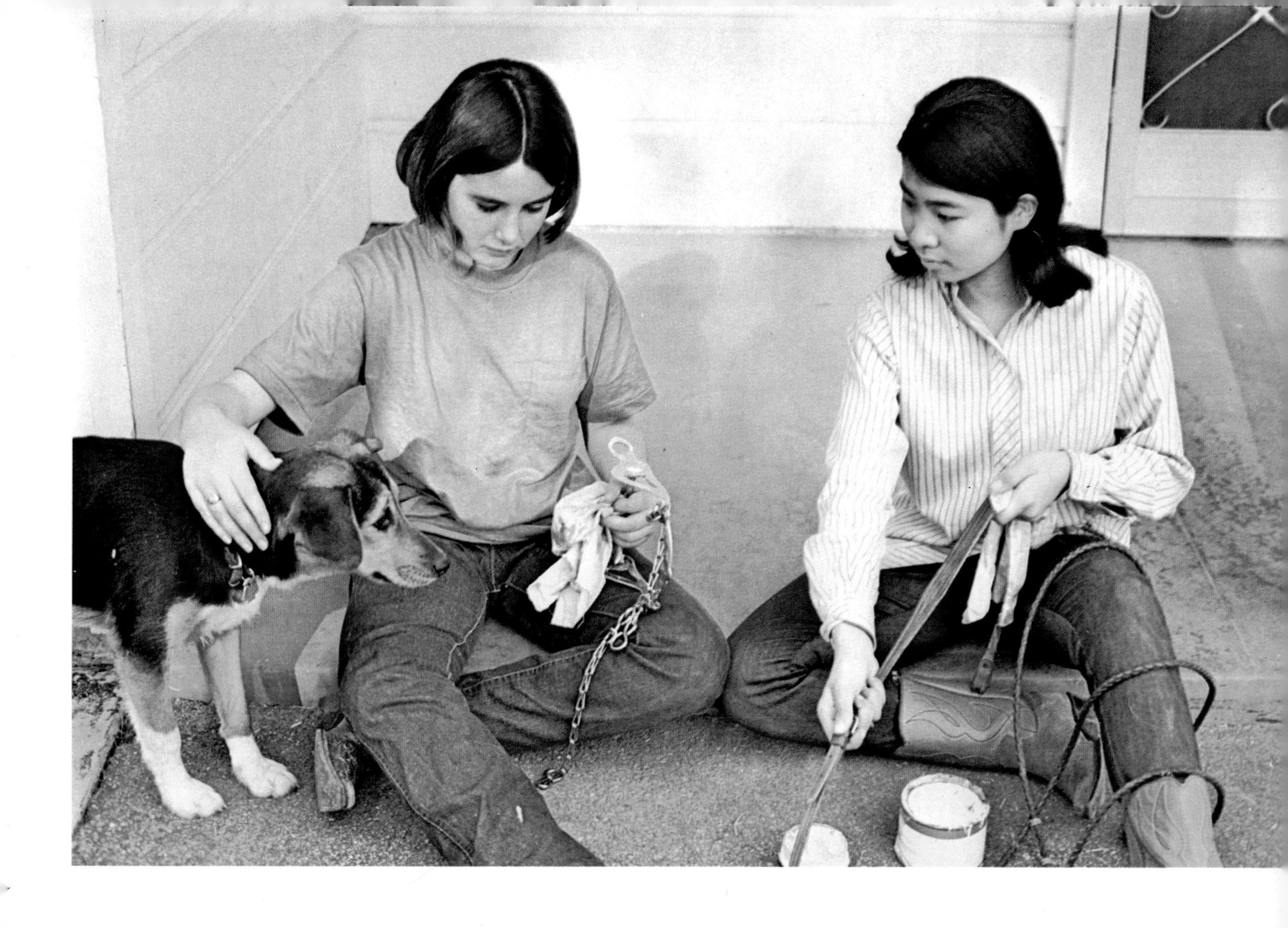

The *bridle* needs cleaning, too. The parts of the bridle are the *bit*, *headstall*, and *reins*. Robin shines the bit, while Joan uses saddle soap to clean the headstall and reins.

At a show the highpoint trophy goes to the rider with the most points. You get points when you win a ribbon. A second place ribbon earns more points than a fourth or fifth. It takes more than luck to win a high point trophy.

Sam likes horse shows when he can walk to them. He doesn't like going in a trailer. A horse trailer means a rough ride, so he always gives an argument. Robin needs friends to help her win the argument.

It's hard to know who is more stubborn, Robin or Sam. But, what horse can stay stubborn when a girl puts grain in the trailer? Sam quits arguing when he smells that grain. Sorry, Sam, you lose!

The horse show starts with Showmanship. You don't ride your horse in Showmanship, but lead him around at a walk and a jog. The judge looks at Sam as if he had five legs, but he is really judging how Robin shows her horse. Smile for the judge, Sam!

Later, they go in a different class, Bareback Horsemanship. It takes balance to ride without saddles in the Bareback Horsemanship class. If you can't balance, don't ride bareback.

Horses don't get flat tires, but they can lose shoes. That's why a horse shoer or *farrier* comes to the show. A farrier can put new shoes on your horse fast enough to keep you riding for ribbons.

The trail class starts at a closed gate. The rider must open the gate while she sits on her horse. She holds the gate and closes it without taking her hand off it, and that's hard!

If you think working the gate is hard, look at this bridge! Robin talks to Sam and presses him with her heels and up he goes over the bridge. Now do you know which one is stubborn?

The judge at the show is a person who knows all about horses and riding. A ring stewardess helps the judge. The ring stewardess gives the announcer signals. From the signals, the announcer knows what to tell the riders to do.

Later the riders line up to hear who wins. Sam always gets sleepy waiting while they announce all the winners. Banner isn't sleepy because he and Joan get a red ribbon for second place.

Wake up, Sam! Whoa, Robin! She nearly gets Sam off balance when she pats his neck to say, "Sam, you won first place!" Do you think Sam is saying, "What's all the fuss about?"

The show is over and Sam seems glad to be back home. After a whole day under a saddle, it must feel good to roll in the dirt. We can be sure Robin and Sam will sleep tonight!

Do you think Sam dreams the same dream Robin does? She dreams about the time on the fourth of July when they won high point trophy. Just think! That was the day Uncle Sam rode Sam!